Evolution of a Black Swallowtail - Larva

C. Antoinette

Presentation by *BookLeaf Publishing*

Web: www.bookleafpub.com

E-mail: info@bookleafpub.com

ISBN: 9789358367393

First edition 2024

Young Delicatessa,

You are the core and the shield. May you always remember that you are The One.

ACKNOWLEDGEMENT

Thank you to God for blessing me with courage and resilience.
Thank you to the dysfunction that taught me love has many languages.
Thank you to my parents for the grand initiation.
Thank you to Renee for hope & inspiration.
Very special thank you to the angels, in human form, who encouraged me to use my voice and to love my light.

PREFACE

Contessa Webster beautifully entwines the evolution of pain with the journey to self-love in part one of this artful trilogy, *Evolution of the Black Swallowtail*. She takes readers through the heartfelt process of hurting, questions, reflection and healing to invoke reminders of love and rites of passage.

Mermaid

She's a Mermaid
swimming among the sharks and
they dig her magic
They
see her enchantment
and get drawn into
extraordinary power
A siren
She sees the waters getting rough and deep
so she dives right in
There is no point in fighting it
the current she floats along in
lets life flow where it must
Transatlantic
Everywhere the moon touches
is hers
She is the pearl in the ocean
Grew too big for the oyster
trying to keep her closed in
She rolled off the deep end
Grew gills and fins;
a backbone
No more jellyfish
She accepted being monstrous
Hunted yet lusted after

Most would never be lucky enough
To have had her
No matter the myths
Her truth will never be captured

Haiku I: Love

Gooey and tasty
Sticking me to you like jam
Sweet yummy and good

Haiku II: Bird

4

When trying to fly
mistaken for an angel
She fell far from grace

Larva

I feel like I have been crawling
on the ground
for a million years
Inching my way through dirt,
grit, mud, storms
scorching suns
There were some pleasant ones
Running my skin over flowers
Most over leaves and spiky thorns
But every once and a while
a hand comes down from the clouds
to choose me
Runs their finger down my spine slowly
To feel how soft I am
To feel me trembling
To feel how scared they can make me
Pluck me from my life
for their pleasantries
Don't feed me or nourish me
Just place me in a box
to define me and forget
that I even exist

Trash

I let him use me
like a receptacle
Toss me around
then out
with the cum rag
like I'm the scumbag
I let him
Treat me like Tupperware
The frosted kind
The kind you think you can see through
Try to devour love before it smells putrid
I keep sniffing and questioning
I don't want to look stupid
but the plastic is too cloudy
and stained with red residue
to get a good view
of the real food
Spoiled real bad
but I'm not the type to hoard
I tend to throw things out cuz
Out of sight means out of mind
Trash collection is at 6 am

Scandal

I was Olivia
No, I wasn't a Saint
I wasn't the Pope
A silly bitch in love
I had a surplus of hope
and forgiveness
Clear water that ran rapid to repentance
In an instant
I was with it
Wherever he went, I visited
A chameleon in his environment
I adapted
to crying and trying again
I knew all the options, but I denied it
Sister-wife-ing it in silence
He was my home, but he had no stability
to share
It didn't matter where he was
I just wanted to be there
It didn't matter what soup I sucked up;
tasteless or sour
I could take it as long as dessert was coming
Waiter! It's been hours! Oh, Waiter!
Still every night I woke up frantic at midnight
looking for the traitor

left to make my own snacks; searching for tea
Because a sad bitch
is always hungry
for something

Stable As a Cloud

Set me out on a voyage to Atlantis
I won't bring a map or an Atlas
Happily lost to be found
I put my crystals on the dashboard
to soak up the sun
Asked them which way was north
but they didn't make a sound
Stuck them in my bra to ride shotgun
Happily lost to be found
As stagnant as a leaf blowing in the wind
Dust and debris flying in my eyes
Random lil pieces
of various dirty men
Stick to the cuffs of my pant hem
Just drag them along on my journey
Let them all fall to the ground
Happily lost to be found

Haiku III: Sins

One day I woke up
Decided that forgiveness
is up to their God

The Element

I'm solar
renewable energy
Sometimes polar
opposite of the crowd
but they're so into me
I live in the clouds
I'm disorderly
You can't order me
I'm like a special edition Casadei
strutting like I own the place
I don't stop to show out or to show face
I'm a seed underground
just waiting patiently to sprout

I'm the Sun and the Water

I'm the moon, on the lake
after kissing someone's daughter
I'm also the gritty sand
Waiting for boats to dock
and feet to land

Assimilation

I'm standing in the middle of this life
It's all happening around me,
but I'm not included
The people I think I know
want me to know
things that I don't
Want me to agree
Want me down on my knees
Yet I'm still standing, whilst not knowing
Clarity averting me
There's socks on the floor
There's the other shoe I was looking for
Who is looking for me?
Is anyone looking for me
besides me?
Beside me is my Self and she's judging
Yesterday she cleaned the bathroom
so today, I need to be on my shit
or she'll put me down
I've been beside myself with doubt for a while
now
At least my shadow is confident
Of course she is
She's the one
that's been doing all the work

Everything is Temporary

Before you a dream
was only something I had swam in
only to drown up the river
With you
Our dreams come true
In the midst of every visit
Costs
feel like investments in your pleasure
Yet you return them all to me
Everything is temporary
Yet you keep coming back to me
Everything is temporary
Yet you keep coming back to see
If this is real
Is this any different
Can we really go the distance but,
Everything is temporary so
we die and go to heaven
before our feet ever hit the floor

Haiku IV: Bookmark

Every time that he
Closes a brand new chapter
He slides me in too

Powerpuff Girl

Black girl
grab your bubble wand
and your bubblicious
your jump rope
and your radio
Join me on the stoop
while I braid my doll baby's hair
and tell me
about the buttercup
you held under your chin
The honeysuckles you're drinking in
The dollar you found on the ground
What you won't be able to do this weekend
Cuz your mama won't be around
What you heard your brother say to that girl on
the phone
All things you aren't gonna do to your kids
When you are grown
How you're gonna be the greatest braider ever
Or maybe a singer or competitive dancer
It's Thursday again
Did you receive your daddy's letter?

Yoga

Bending this way
twisting that
Will leave you with a lumbar spine
But very little memory of
how to hold your head up

Hunting Season

Lucky you,
Caught me in the peak season of my trauma
I let you treat me like trash
Practically handed you the bag
to stuff me in to
I made sure it was the flexible kind
Heftier than Hefty
Cause everything you put out there
was flimsy and unreliable
You didn't care if I spilled out onto the street
As long as it wasn't visible from your window
or lain out on your lawn
I wasn't something you wanted to go thru
Just something you wanted at your disposal

Sunshine the Leo

He is the sun
Igniting a ravishing fire
That burns through me
Heating my core
The center of life-giving energy
Intimacy
He sees into me and
awakening curiosity's mystery
I need it like he restoreth my soul
So he lays down with me
where the grass is always greener
I plant flowers
and bring him some

When it's my time to shine
Floral pastures
are his resting place
Soft dark clouds
floating in his face
resting in his hands
Kissing his cheeks and forehead

Just like the moon
I shine and smile down on him
He sips sweet nectar

to my lullabies
Rubbing on my black hourglass
like I have unlimited wishes to grant
for a limited time only
When he dreams
He dreams of me
eyes wide open wide
Dusk til dawn is when it's the wettest
Dew forms all over everything
I gently rock him to sleep
til he rises in the morning
and we do it all over again

Haiku IV - Phoenix

20

A Phoenix never
Emerges from death without
some scars and singes

Haiku V

If I make you feel
Good in and out of the bed
You can have both sides

PTSD

Ptsd
Had me thrown off my frequency
Been in a depression ever since
I let a lowly obscurity
handle me
Not usually
It musta been a trauma response
I loved that the touch felt so raw
I hate that it cost me so much
Magic in exchange
for ole ordinary
Lust

Fonder

I love it when you love me
The way it feels
being curled up beside you
Wrapped up inside you
I feel safe in your arms
You make me forget deadlines
and who owes me money

I already pulled up the bathroom rugs
to sweep the floor but
you make me want to leave them in the hallway

I love it when you love me
When all you do is to please me
I do my hair and you see me
You tell me that I'm pretty
Everything feels so easy
Time with you feels short
and new

I love it when our fingers intertwine
Just like our lips do
They hug together tightly
mimicking you and I
Feels better when
we haven't seen each other in a while

Untitled

You don't validate efforts or feelings
but I get to park in your complex for free
I would hate to meet you there
and you tell me I had to leave
Better grab all my things
my pillow and my keys
at once